NOTTINGHAM DIALECT

A selection of words and anecdotes
from around Nottinghamshire

by
Natalie Braber

BRADWELL
BOOKS

Published by Bradwell Books
9 Orgreave Close Sheffield S13 9NP
Email: books@bradwellbooks.co.uk

British Library Cataloguing in Publication Data:
a catalogue record for this book is available from the
British Library.

1st Edition

ISBN: 9781909914735

Design and artwork by: Andrew Caffrey

Print: Gomer Press, Llandysul, Ceredigion SA44 4JL

Image Credits: Shutterstock
and credited individually

NOTTINGHAMSHIRE DIALECT

by Natalie Braber

ACKNOWLEDGEMENTS

This book was written at the request of Chris Gilbert. I would like to thank him for this. I would also like to thank all those people who have inspired me with examples of Nottinghamshire dialect. They also gave me many laughs along the way. Thanks also to 'Picture the Past' for allowing me to use some of their photos of the region and to Nottingham Local Studies library for letting me use their oral history collection. I would also like to thank Norma Braber-McKinney for her photos that are used in this volume. Thanks to those who have helped me find information and checked facts when I needed help: David Amos, Ben Braber, Jayne Carroll, Becca Gregory, Christina Raven Conn and Jonnie Robinson. This book is dedicated to Leon and Finn, who are always there to explore new Nottinghamshire places with me.

Introduction

I have lived in Nottingham for almost ten years now. When I first moved here – after living in Amsterdam, Glasgow, St Andrews, Berlin and Manchester – the language used by the local people and all its wonderful sounds quickly started to fascinate me. This language was obviously different to the other varieties of English that I had come across before, or indeed used myself! There were influences from the way people use language in the north of England while at the same time I heard features that I would expect to hear in more southern varieties of English. One of the first things I did in Nottingham was going into a 'Cob Shop' just to see what they sold there, because 'cob', used like that, was a word I had never come across before!

I moved to Nottingham to work as a linguist at Nottingham Trent University. Much of my work means looking into language and identity as well as the use of emotion in language. When I decided to see what research had been carried out about my new home town and Nottinghamshire, I found there was very little, and almost nothing written by academics. This was really interesting: it suggested that this variety of language was either not worth studying, or not considered sufficiently different to other regions. Neither of these two possibilities I believed to be true. And ever since this time I have been working on language in the East Midlands. Some people believe that the language used in Nottinghamshire can be hard to recognise. Or they find it difficult to pinpoint where exactly people use it – particularly for people who are not from the area. Some local dialect books even mention examples of words and sentences written without spaces between them, to show how confusing it can be. In this book, I have tried to gather information from many different fields of interest that symbolise Nottinghamshire – children's games, life at home, and work in the coalmines, farms and factories. I have also looked at well-known books from this part of the world. In such a small volume, there is of course not scope to cover everything. Some of you may feel that essential subjects have been missed. However, I hope this book gets you talking and makes for an entertaining read.

Merry Men Norma Braber-McKinney

Dialect Dictionary

A

Aas/Ahs – house

Abaht – about

Afore – before

Afto – afternoon

Again – next to, beside

Agen – against

Ah'll go to Trent – an expression of surprise

Aht – out

Allers/Allus – always

Annall – also

Appen – perhaps or that is so (*'Appen Sir Clifford 'ud know'* from D.H. Lawrence)

Apple-in-and-out – traditional Nottingham pudding made with apple and batter

A'ready – already

Ax – ask

Ay – yes

B

Babby – baby

Back-end weather – autumnal weather

Badly – hungover or ill

Bank – coal face

Barney – argument

Bat – hit

Batchy – dim

Battle-twig – earwig

Beer-off – off licence

Bellyband – girth for fastening saddle onto a horse

Belt job – easy job (such as sleeping while watching the conveyor belt)

Beskad – Bestwood Park

Besom stave – broom handle, see also *steyl*

Bin – been (for example, *ow's you bin*)

Bird tenting – to scare birds away using a clapper or rattle

Blather-yeded – silly person

Bleddy – bloody

Blether – chat

Bliddaf – Blidworth

Blooer – noise cows (cahs) and bulls make

Blortin' – crying

Blubber – to cry uncontrollably

Bluey – blewit mushroom

Bobbar – please don't touch

Bobbo – horse

Bod – bird

Bodge up – repair something and having to make do with what you have

Bogger – fool (from '*bugger*'). This is a mild and affectionate word and has no sexual connotations. It may come from an Middle English word *bugge*, meaning imaginary monster.

Bonny – plump or slightly overweight

Borrow – lend (*borrow me your new dress*), see also lend

Bostin' – desperate for (*bostin' for the toilet*)

Boz-eyed – cross-eyed

Braghast – mischievous child

Brassic – to have no money whatsoever

Bread and Lard Island – West Bridgford (it is said by some that people who live there live beyond their means to keep up appearances)

Brew – a cup of tea

Brushing – trim field hedges

Bubblin' – baby bird still in nest

Bunghole – cheese (*bread and bunghole*)

Butty – job title for worker in pit, a sub-contractor who was in charge of a particular group of miners

C

Cadge – borrow

Cage – lift in mine shaft, see also chair

Caggy (also cag-handed) – left-handed, see also *keggy-handed*

Canna – cannot

Cap off – skip school

Causey/corsey – pavement

Chair – lift taken into the mine, see also cage

Chapel 'at pegs (bones or eyes) – someone who is either thin or staring at you with wide-open eyes

Chara – horse-drawn vehicle, or open motor vehicle (generally for sight-seeing purposes), short for *charabanc*

Charlie – ladies' underskirt

Charlie's dead – warning to let someone know their underskirt is showing

Chelp – answer back cheekily

Chikin' – peeping through curtains

Chimbley – chimney

Chuffed – pleased

Chunter – mutter something under your breath

Clammed – very hungry indeed

Cleat – wooden wedge to prop things up or stop them moving down the pit

Clout – to hit hard

Clouts/claarts – trousers

Cob – bread roll

Cobbles – medium-sized bits of coal

Cock – local form of address (particularly among men)

Cock on a stick – traditional lollies sold at the Goose Fair

Cockwood – wood brought home from the mine to please the wife

Coggin – apple core

Collier – miner

Come yowe! – farmer's call to sheep

Conk – a lookout (*to keep conk*)

Colly nobs (also known as nobi greens) – Brussels sprouts

Copper – drum used for washing clothes

Coppy – group of small trees growing together

Cot – pigsty

Cotted hair – knotty hair, see also *lugs*

Cow lady – ladybird

Cowd – cold

Clo'es – clothes

Croaker – doctor

Croggie – a ride on the crossbars of a bike

Cum – come

Cup cup – farmer's call to horses

Cush cush – farmer's call to cows

D

Dahn – down

Dannies – baby's hands

Derby Road – cold (rhyming slang)

Dicks – head lice

Didna – Did not

Dobby – game like tig where children had to try and catch each other

Dog chalk – chalk used for drawing hopscotch lines

Dool-owls – poor souls

Dot'ill – slag tip at the pit

Dotty – dirty

Down th'pit – In the mine

Duck – a term of endearment or greeting used for everyone, young or old, male or female, known or unknown

Duck's necks – bottle of lemonade

Duddoos – sweets

Dudley – water bottle (used by some miners)

Dunna – do not

E

Eck – hell (*what the eck!*)

Eerd – heard

Ellzly – Elkesley

Errywosh – Erewash (used for both the valley and the river)

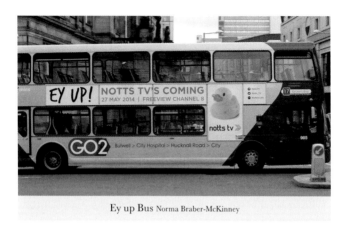

Ey up Bus Norma Braber-McKinney

Ey up! – a greeting, often used with duck: *Ey up mi duck!*
Eyya gorrowt? – have you got anything?

F

Face like a bag of frogs – someone who is rather unattractive
Fahl-ahs – hen house
Faither – father
Fast – stuck or caught
Faunt – found
Fawce – sly
Fer – for
Fib it – to hide something discreetly
Firedamp – methane (in the pit)

Flicks – cinema

Flit – move house (often secretly in the night if avoiding debt collectors!), also used for moving coal

Foller – follow

Forest (aka The Reds) – Nottingham Forest Football Club

Forpni mix – portion of chips with mushy peas

Fossneck – a know-it-all

Fost – first

Fortherum – hay loft

Fou – unattractive

Fret – worry

Frit – scared

Funneh – funny

Fust – first

G

Gadding – going about in a flippant way

Gaffer – boss

Gangin' – pony riding in the coal mine

Ganzie – jumper

Gartman – man who looks after cows

Gate – entrance shafts in and out of mine (these gates had many different names in different pits – Names for entry shaft: number one shaft, supply gate, feeder gate, loader gate, main gate, mother gate; names for exit shaft: number two shaft, supply gate, tail gate)

Gee – to turn right when ploughing with horses (see also *hauve*)

Gel – girl

Gen – to give

Gerraht! – I don't believe it!

Gerron – get on (*gerron wi' it*)

Gerr o't on it! – go away!

Gi' – to give (*gi' it me*)

Gilt – young female pig

Gimmers – sheep

Ginnel/Gennel – walkway between terraced houses

Gizza gleg! – let's have a look

Gizzagoo – it is my turn now

Gleg – to look at in a nosey fashion

Goatum – Gotham

Gobbins – waste area in the pit (also you want *gobbin'* – you deserve to be thrown away)

Gobbo – wet cement or mortar

Goosy – the goose of the Goose Fair, an annual travelling fair which visits Nottingham in the first week of October

Gormless – insane

Gormy – slow on the uptake

Grett – great, big (for example '*Yo and yo' bloody grett clodhoppers*' from ALAN SILLITOE)

Gumption – common sense

Guzgogs – gooseberries

Guzzunder – commode (under bed pot)

H

Hanks – skein of silk or other material

Ha-porth – half-penny's worth

Hark – look, for example *hark at them lot*

Harrow – heavy timber frame with iron teeth which was ploughed over land to break up clods of earth

Hauve – to turn left when ploughing with horses (see also *gee*)

Have a cob on – to be in a mood

Have a green one – throw a sick day

Have a munk on – to be in a mood

Hiding – a beating or thrashing

Hissen/'Issen – himself

Hottie – hot water bottle

I

Idle Jacks (also idlebacks) – loose skin around fingernails

Island – roundabout

J

Jasper – wasp

Jiggered – exhausted
Jitty – alley behind houses (often closed at one end)
Jollop – medicine
Jono? – do you realise?

K

Kayleye – sherbert
Keggy-handed – left-handed (also clumsy), see also *caggy*
Kekks – trousers
Kittle – to have kittens (of a cat! So not meaning someone being angry about something)
Klawkin' – cat scratching something
Knock on/off – referring to the shuttle on a lace machine where levers were knocked on and off by hand
Knocker upper – someone who would knock on windows to waken those without alarm clocks
Knocking on – dating

L

Lad – term for male, also used by miners when addressing younger men
Lairy – loud
Larup – cover with a thick substance, like butter or margarine on bread

Las' – last

Lass – girl or young woman

Learn – to teach (*I've learnt them that*)

Lend – to borrow (*you can lend my shoes*), see also *borrow*

Len'n – Lenton

Ligger – liar

Little pigs have big ears – careful, children might be overhearing!

Livin' in tally – unmarried couple living together, see also *over the brush*

Lolly – money

Look at someone gone out – to look at someone in a confused manner as if they have said something ridiculous

Lugs – knots in hair: luggy hair, see also *cotted hair*

Lummox – idiot

M

Ma'e – make, see also *mek*

Magpies – Notts County Football Club

Mam – Mum

Manny – argumentative

Mappleh – Mapperley

Mardy – moody, grumpy

Mash – make tea

Mawks – maggots (*liftin' wi' mawks* refers to something, for example meat, that is crawling with maggots)

Mawl – mallet used by farmers

Mazzgi – cat (particularly in Sneinton, St Anns and the Meadows)

Mazzi-watter – said of weak beer: *it's like mazzi-watter*

Meddalain – Notts County football stadium

Medders/Meddas – Meadows

Meet you at the left lion – popular meeting spot outside the Council House on Market Square in Nottingham

Mek – make, see also *ma'e*

Mesen – myself

Mither – to moan (as in *stop mithering*)

Mizzle – very fine rain

Moggy – usually cat, but also mouse in some areas of Nottinghamshire

Moldiwarp – mole

Mucky – dirty

Mun – must

Munna – must not

Munney – money

Left Lion Norma Braber-McKinney

18

N

Nah – now

Naight – night

Nanar – grandmother (this particular intonation is very particular to this region, and very different to nanna which is also found in other parts of the country)

Nannight – goodnight/sleep well

Nark – to tell on someone

Nay – no

Nebbeh – nosy

Nedna – needn't

Nesh – someone who feels the cold

Netty – toilet (used originally by Geordie miners, but word use spread)

Nicky 'at – Trilby hat

Niver – never

Noo – new

Noodles – cuddles

Nowt (also pronounced as *note* by some) – nothing, for example *there's nowt wrong wi' me*, see also *owt*

Nunnoos – money given to children

Nuts – small bits of coal

O

Oakey – ice cream (Oakey man to refer to the ice cream van)

O'Grady says – 'Simon says' game, where children have to copy a ringleader, apart from if they don't start the sentence with *O'Grady says* and then they aren't to copy them

Ollin' it dahn – raining very heavily, see also *silin' dahn* and *teem*

Omm – home

On the panel – to have a doctor's note

On'y – only

Oppo – friend

Os – horse

Otch otch – farmer's call to chickens

Our – affectionate term in relation to family member, for example our mam or our followed by person's name

Ourn – ours

Over Bill's Mother – over there (*It's black over Bill's mother* meaning that it is likely to rain soon)

Over the brush – living together unmarried, see also *livin' in tally*

Ovver t'brook – name given to those living on the Nottinghamshire side of the Erewash by those on the Derbyshire side, sometimes also referred to as *'wrong side o't' brook'!*

Owd – old

Owd up! – be careful!

Owdya orsuzz! – please be patient!

Owja sweat! – take it easy!

Owt (also pronounced ote by some) – something/anything, see also *nowt*

Oyya-beya-sen? – are you alone?

P

Peas – coal slack

Pen-toed – pigeon toed

Pewit – lapwing

Piddle – falling liquid (like rain or urine, *it's piddlin' dahn*, or *havin' a piddle*)

Piggle – to pick at a scab or spot

Pissmire – ant

Pit – mine

Plait rain – do miracles (if you can do that, you can plait rain)

Pleece – police

Pobs – stale bread soaked in tea

Pods – boottees

Poddle – to amble

Ponch – used for pushing down on clothes while in tub (see *copper*) to wash them before washing machines were widely used

Pot – plaster cast
Pots – dishes
Puddled – drunk
Put wood in t'ole – close the door
Puther – ooze out

Q

Queen o't' Midlands – Nottingham (those in Leicester may argue with this term!)

R

Rag up – miner putting outer clothes back on after a shift
Rammel – nonsense (or worthless rubbish), particularly in the sense of owd rammel, also used for waste material in the pit
Rawky – misty
Recklin' – youngest pig of a litter
Reesty – rancid meat
Reet/reight – right (*it'll be reet*)
Rigg – raised part of ploughed field
Rime – frosting of ice on objects
Robin Hood's rhubarb – burdock
Rope walk – stretch of ground where ropes are made, as a result the Rope Walk in Nottingham city centre

Rosy apple (also known as spirit tapping) – knocking on someone's door and running away

Rustica bomm – version of the children's game leapfrog

S

Safto – this afternoon

The Salutation – Ye Olde Salutation Inn, a pub in Nottingham city centre

Sat'day/Satdy – Saturday

Savoury ducks – faggots (meal made with meat off-cuts)

Scraitin' – crying

Scrat – thin spread on bread

Scrike – to cry

Scruffs – work clothes

Serry – name for someone who is a friend

Shovel-footed – splay-footed

Shuki lam – lamp used for poaching

Shurrup – be quiet

Shut on – get rid of

Sick road – once a roundabout has been turning one way for a while, when the direction is reversed it is said to be *on the sick road*

Silin' dahn – very heavy rain, see also *ollin' it dahn* and *teem*

Since – ago (ten years since)

Sithee – bye bye

Sitti Grahnd – Nottingham Forest football stadium

Skank – mean or unfair

Sket – useless person

Skinny – mean

Skreeton (or Skrayton) – Screveton

Slaip – sleep

Slape – slippery (of roads especially)

Sludgebump – someone put upon by others

Snap – lunch, initially especially used by miners but now widespread

Snap tin – lunch box

Snap time – lunch time

Sneck – door handle

Snen'n – Sneinton

Snided – many (for example, *snided with ants*, or in the sense of busy, as in *fair snided out with folk*)

Snobs – children's game with stones

Sorrey (also spelt surry) – a term of familiarity, often used by miners

Sowjers – soldiers

Spadger – sparrow

Speckles – freckles

Spink – to tell a fib

Spink – chaffinch

Splodge – to kiss

Sprag open – to prop open a door

Sprog – baby pigeon

Staavin' – very cold (of weather)

Stabbo – Stapleford

Staddle – base of haystack

Standing – stall in a stable

Starnel/Stahnal – starling

Steyl – broom handle, see also *besom stave*

Stickin' – collecting firewood

Stint – workplace in the mine

Stop with – stay with

Sucker – ice lolly

Summat – something

Sup – a drink

Suthell – Southwell (or is it?)

Swaftin' – swimming

Swaller – swallow (used by some to mean to drink)

Swank – to brag or boast

Sweatin' cobs – to feel rather warm

Swiggin' – drinking (especially alcohol)

Swoal-edded – arrogant

T

T' – the

Ta ta – bye bye, see also *tarr-ar*

Tab – ear

Tab 'angin' – eavesdropping

Ta'e – take, see also *tek*

Tagging – topping and tailing swedes

Tansy – a pudding made of fruit puree

Tarr-ar – bye bye, see also *ta ta*

Tates – potatoes

T'ave – to have

Teem – to pour down with rain, see also *ollin' it dahn* and *silin' dahn*

Teggies – teeth (especially used when referring to children's teeth)

Tek – take, see also *ta'e*

Telt – told

Ter – to (for example *'e's got far ter go*)

Termorrer/Tomorrer – tomorrow

Tha – you

Thee – you

Theirn – theirs

Think on – think of

Thissen – themselves

Thosty – thirsty

Thowt – thought

Throng – busy

Thuzda – Thursday

Thoty – thirty

Threp'ney rush (also referred to as tuppenny rush) –
day when children's films were showing at the cinema

Thysen – yourself

Tin-a-lurky – children's game kicking a tin down
the street

Tit – small horse

Toddy – small

Togs – work clothes worn in the pit

Tother – the other

Towd – told

t'Trip – Ye Olde Trip to Jerusalem, a pub in Nottingham
city centre

Tub – coal wagon used in the mine

Tucks – fits of laughter

Tuffey – toffee (as in *tuffey apples*) but also used for sweets
generally

Tups – sheep

T'was – it was

Tweggies – straps worn around miners' trousers to stop
dust getting in

Twitchell – narrow passage or alley behind houses
(open at both ends)

Twist – spoonfuls of tea twisted in newspaper

U

Uckna – Hucknall

Udge up – move over

Us – me, for example show us it

Us – our

V

Vexed – annoyed

W

Wain't – won't

Wakes – annual local holiday period, usually two weeks in summer when factory workers received holiday leave

Waller – tasteless meat

Wash yer tabs out – pay attention, listen carefully!

Watter – water

Wazzerk (also spelt wassock) – fool

Wellows – Wellington boots

Weshas – wash house, often outside the back of the house where people and clothes could be washed

We's'll – we shall

Wezzle-brained – foolish

Wheer – where

Whittle – worry unnecessarily

Wi' – with

Wi'out – without

Winder – window

Windows – glasses

Wiser – Wysall

Wok – work

Wor (it wor) – it is or it was

Worra yer on wi'? – what are you doing?

Worn't – it wasn't

Wow – noise cats make

Wunna – won't

Y

Yack – to throw

Yawpin' – complaining

Y'd berra tell 'er t' gerrit 'er sen! – you had better tell her to get it herself!

Yer – you and your

Yo' – you

Yoursen – yourself

Yourn – yours

Youth – like 'mate', especially used by miners for men of all ages

Nottinghamshire Memories

Someone who worked on hosiery frames:

That's when I started in the hosiery, I went silk winding fust on nights, to keep the silk, they used it fer the stockings, you know women's stockings, they'd got six machines meking them and I had to keep em going winding this silk on to bobbins off hanks, well then they got one or two more knitting machines and as I say they put me on these knitting machines and that's where I learned me trade, and you did learn it there because the gaffer, he was a terrible, wicked man, and you knew, you knew you'd got to be right, you was scared stiff on him.

Domestic work:

Well, I used to have to help me mother. Oh yes, because, as I say, there was a lot to do, and on a washday it was always a very big day, because there'd be eight of us to wash for, so it was – of course there was none of these modern washers and all that sort of thing – old-fashioned ponches, but we got through very well.

Blackleading:

Well first of all we used to wipe the grate down and then we got the blacklead and brushed it on with a brush, that was the blacklead brush which was a rather long one about six inches long and round at the end. Then we had a brush for polishing which was a flat brush, more like a hairbrush of today, but it was for polishing blacklead, and it used to come up beautiful, this was done at regular intervals. And the floor of that part of the house wasn't concrete it was red bricks and they were scrubbed regular and cleaned.

Victoria Market:

'*In its early days there used to be coach trips from outlying districts used to come to visit the Victoria Centre because it was such a fascinating thing. I mean, it's the biggest shopping centre at that time in Europe. It certainly was the most modern and to be able to shop under ideal conditions whatever the time of the year it was, and you kept dry in the wet days, you kept cool in the hot days, it was a big attraction*'.

Victoria Market (when the market first started up in the Victoria Centre in 1972)

Pronunciation and Usage

English has changed during the past few centuries and older varieties would sound like a foreign language to us. In Anglo-Saxon times, England had four main dialects, which differed greatly from each other. One of these was Mercian. This was spoken in the area that nowadays includes both the East and West Midlands. Much of this influence remains visible today. Many East Midlands dialects owe a lot of their grammar and vocabulary to Nordic influences, because this region was part of the Danelaw in the ninth century.

It is said that people in Nottinghamshire like to talk loudly. Some material in this book has been gained from tab-'angin'. You need good breath control to speak it, because there are very few pauses between words in sentences. This can also make the language spoken here hard to understand for outsiders. It is important to remember, though, that there is plenty of variation within Nottinghamshire too – a miner from Mansfield will speak differently from a factory worker in Nottingham or a farmer in Newark. Plus, men and women may use language in different ways, and children may speak differently to their parents (and grandparents).

The English language will continue to change. And it will do so greatly in Nottinghamshire, where many of the traditional industries have disappeared or are in the process of vanishing. There are always new people moving into the region both from within and outside the UK. This diversity will add many new features to the language. So this book tries to record some of what Nottinghamshire used to sound like. It will take you from ey up mi duck to tarr-ar and focus on topics that are likely to be useful as they are important to the region – from sport and pastimes to work and interaction with others.

Place Names

There are many places names in Nottinghamshire that show different historical influences. Some of these influences are from Anglo-Saxon times. For example, the ending field as in Mansfield or Ashfield comes from an Anglo-Saxon word meaning 'open ground'. The ending by, as in Thoresby, is thought to come from the Danish word for 'town'. Some names are humorous (a nickname for West Bridgford is Bread and Lard Island, in the sense that the people who live there need to scrimp and save to keep up appearances with the neighbours!). Or simply nice such as Bunny, which comes from the Old English 'dry ground in a marsh where reeds grow'.

Some place names are confusing. Beeston has nothing to do with bees, but is likely to come from Old English meaning 'the farmstead where bent grass is seen'. Some place names are pronounced in a typical local way which can be confusing for others, such as Stabbo (Stapleford), Meddas (The Meadows), Beskad (Bestwood Park), Bliddaf or Bliduth (Blidworth), Skreeton (Screveton) and Uckna (Hucknall).

Nottingham

In Anglo-Saxon times, around AD 600, the site of present-day Nottingham formed part of the Kingdom of Mercia. It was known as 'Tigguo Cobauc', meaning 'a place of cave dwellings'. You can find the earliest evidence of the city in the form more familiar to us today in the late ninth century, where it is described as Snotengaham. It appears in the Domesday records as Snotingeham. This is likely to have come from the original Saxon words where the inge appears in place names and follows a person's name and means 'the people or followers of'. So the name Snotingeham means 'the homestead of Snot's people'. This person is also likely to have given his name to Sneinton. For Nottingham, thankfully, the initial letter 'S' was dropped in the 12th century owing to Norman influence. Although some towns and villages return to their original names, it is safe to say that this is unlikely to happen in the case of Nottingham.

The city's motto is *'Vivit post funera virtus'* which means *'Virtue outlives death'*.

Southwell

Southwell is most famously home to Southwell Minster. The earliest record of a church on this site dates from as early as 627. It is also home of the Bramley apple. The origins of the name come from the Old English meaning 'the place at the south spring'. Although this fact is relatively uncontroversial, the pronunciation of the name is not! The debate continues to rage about whether the town should be pronounced 'Southwell' or 'Suthull'. Some people say that locals call it 'Southwell', but that those outside the town call it 'Suthull'. Others say it is to do with snobbiness (with 'Suthull' said to be more posh). The BBC originally only gave the pronunciation 'Suthull' but now uses both as possible options. The controversy is set to continue, with disagreements both in the town and outside it.

Southwell Minster Shutterstock/Tony Brindley

While you are visiting Southwell, don't miss the Minster. There you can try to spot the twelve wooden mice carved by Robert 'Mouseman' Thompson, a British furniture maker whose trademark was to carve a mouse on almost every single item he made.

Gotham

This village is not pronounced in the same way as the Gotham City of the Batman films, but as 'Goatum'. It comes from the Saxon gat + ham, meaning 'goat homestead'. An interesting story about Gotham concerns the Wise Men of Gotham. There are around twenty of these stories and they first appeared in print in 1540. They recount some of the ways in which the citizens of Gotham convinced King John they were mad. Some people say they did this to avoid having to make the village road a public highway for his journey through the village, which they would have to pay taxes for. Others claim that they wanted to prevent the king building a hunting lodge nearby, because that would stop the villagers being able to hunt in the area.

In the tale *'The Kind Master'* a man rides his horse carrying a sack of corn on his own shoulder in order to relieve the burden on his horse. Another of the tales, *'The Cuckoo Bush of Gotham'*, has villagers building a hedge around a tree to entrap a cuckoo. When the bird flies off, the villagers berate themselves for not making the hedge higher. In *'The Drowning of the Gotham Eel'* the villagers punish an eel by drowning it, because they believe it is responsible for killing their fish.

As it was feared that such insanity was contagious, King

John and his men are said to have fled from the village, leaving the villagers portrayed as heroes who managed to outwit the King. The tales of Gotham's wise men belong to a style of folk tales that developed in reaction to the heavy taxation of King John. The best known of these are the tales of Robin Hood, an outlaw who evaded paying taxes, thus also outwitting the apparently greedy monarch.

To commemorate the 800th anniversary of the villager's victory over the king, a weathervane depicting some of the tales has recently been erected in Gotham. There is also a well-known poem describing these wise men:

Three wise men of Gotham,
They went to sea in a bowl,
And if the bowl had been stronger
My song had been longer

Writers and Books

I have to mention some of Nottinghamshire's famous writers and their books. Nottinghamshire was the home of LORD BYRON, D.H. LAWRENCE and ALAN SILLITOE as well as many modern authors, such as the crime writers DAVID BELBIN and RAYMOND FLYNN. For many of these writers, Nottinghamshire landscapes and language form an important part of their writing.

D.H. Lawrence

DAVID HERBERT LAWRENCE, born in 1885, was the son of a former schoolteacher and a Nottinghamshire coalminer. He was brought up in the small mining community of Eastwood at a time when modern industry was transforming the East Midlands countryside. Many of his works were heavily inspired by the local Nottinghamshire countryside. His best-known works are his novels *Sons and Lovers, The Rainbow, Women in Love* and the controversial *Lady Chatterley's Lover*. Much of his work was controversial because of explicit sexual content, particularly *Lady Chatterley's Lover*. This novel became the centre of a famous indecency trial, marking an important change in public views on censorship and the arts. Lawrence also wrote poetry, short stories and essays. He painted and travelled widely. However, the writer retained a deep feeling for his native Nottinghamshire – which he called 'the country of my heart'.

A major theme in his work was the changing countryside and the effect of such changes on the people who lived there. In *Lady Chatterley's Lover*, Connie, Lady Chatterley, is married to Clifford. At the very beginning of the book, there is a comment on the working people of the local village, Wragby.

Clifford professed to like Wragby better than London. This country had a grim will of its own, and the people had guts. Connie wondered what else they had: certainly neither eyes nor minds. The people were as haggard, shapeless, and dreary as the countryside, and as unfriendly. Only there was something in their deep-mouthed slurring of the dialect, and the thresh-thresh of their hob-nailed boots as they trailed home in gangs on the asphalt from work, that was terrible and a bit mysterious.

Much of the novel contrasts the Standard English of the written prose and the voice of the narrator, the upper-class Connie, with the language used by the working people, and specifically the gamekeeper, Mellors, who becomes Connie's lover.

Alan Sillitoe

Far from the rural landscape of Connie and Mellors is the writing of ALAN SILLITOE. He was born in Nottingham in 1928 to working-class parents, and started work at the Raleigh bicycle factory when he left school at 14. His most famous works are *Saturday Night and Sunday Morning* and *The Loneliness of the Long-Distance Runner*. But he also wrote poetry and children's literature. Much of his work is about working-class heroes with a cause. Nottingham and the working-class family are a frequent focus of Sillitoe's work. The protagonist of *Saturday Night and Sunday Morning*, Arthur Seaton, also works at the Raleigh factory. Much of this book features local dialect and Sillitoe makes many references to local events, such as Goose Fair.

The following extract tells how Arthur is able to treat his little nephew to some sweets because of the good money he earns at the factory.

> *We's'll see 'f Taylors 'ave some tuffeys, shall we? But you're a bit of a lead weight, our Bill. What does Margaret feed you on? Cannonballs? Ye'r a ton-weight, and no mistake. The tuffeys wain't mek yer any lighter. I do know that!*

Sillitoe joined the RAF and after being pensioned off, due to tuberculosis, he spent much of his life travelling the world. He was particularly celebrated in Russia, where he was seen to act as a spokesman for the oppressed working-class man.

And just to finish…

Although there are many local authors and lots of stories that could be told from a Nottinghamshire perspective, it seems apt to finish on a limerick. This particular one also reflects local dialect:

A Notts lass on 'oliday in Sicily
Were reight fon o' meyt as were gristly.
When she fun for 'er snap
A piece too gret for 'er trap
She 'id it beneath 'er cam-is-ol-e

A Taste of Nottinghamshire

Much of Nottinghamshire is now a truly multi-cultural mix of people and this is reflected in the restaurants and shops of the region. Many nationalities are represented in food outlets, and tastes have certainly changed from more traditional fare. It is possible to eat in a Michelin-starred restaurant (Sat Bains) or be spoiled in Hart's or World Service. Nottinghamshire is also home to a host of food and drink festivals and local produce is highly valued. There are some local delicacies and traditional recipes, which are celebrated in the region and still consumed by many.

Bramley Apple

Southwell is internationally renowned for the Bramley apple. It was here that it first grew from pips more than 200 years ago in the garden of Mary Ann Brailsford's cottage on Church Street. The tree was later included in the 1846 purchase of the cottage by a local butcher, Matthew Bramley. In 1856, the owner of a local tree nursery, Henry

Merryweather, asked if he could take cuttings from the tree and start to sell the apples. Bramley agreed but insisted that the apples should bear his name. In 1900 the original tree was knocked over during violent storms; it survived, however, and is still bearing fruit two centuries after it was planted. Today it is the most important cooking apple in the United Kingdom. In 2009 a window commemorating the 200th anniversary of the planting of the tree was installed in Southwell Minster.

Bramley apple Shutterstock/Sarah Marchant

Every year in October people gather in Southwell to celebrate the UK's favourite cooking apple, at the Bramley Apple Festival. Music and Morris dancing accompanies eating and drinking. You can also visit the Bramley Apple Inn, which can be found just a few doors away from the original tree.

Bramley apples work well in apple pies and crumbles and as part of a traditional Nottingham pudding, apple-in-and-out, which consists of apples folded in a batter blanket with a crisp top and a soft centre. These apples can also be combined with Merryweather damsons (also developed in Southwell); but do not use guzgogs to make a tansy, a buttered fruit puree made with eggs and breadcrumbs.

Here is the recipe for **Apple-in-and-out** – this should be enough to feed six people.

6 Bramley cooking apples
75g/3oz butter
75g/3oz soft brown sugar
½ teaspoon ground nutmeg
1 teaspoon ground cinnamon
175g/6oz plain flour
Water
3 eggs, beaten
Salt
450ml/¾ pint milk

1. Pre-heat the oven to 200°C/400°F/Gas Mark 6.
2. Peel and core the apples. Cream the butter and sugar, and add the nutmeg and cinnamon. Fill the centre of each apple with the mixture. Place the apples in a large

well-buttered ovenproof dish. It should be a deep dish, with the top of the apples level with its rim, then the batter should rise up and cover the apples during the cooking process.

3. Blend the flour with a little cold water and add the well-beaten eggs to it with a pinch of salt and sufficient milk to make a thick creamy batter. Pour the batter over the apples and bake the pudding in the pre-heated oven for 40 to 50 minutes, until the apples are soft and the batter is risen, gold brown and crisp. Serve immediately, with cream or custard.

Stilton Cheese

If you are still feeling a bit clammed, Stilton is a blue bunghole made in two varieties, Blue and White. It is known as 'The King of Cheeses'. Both types have been granted the status of a protected designation of origin by the European Commission, two of only ten British cheeses currently produced to have such protection. This means that only cheese produced in the three counties of Derbyshire, Leicestershire and Nottinghamshire, made according to a strict code with local pasteurised milk, can be called Stilton. In Nottinghamshire, there are only two dairies that can produce Stilton – the Colston Bassett Dairy and the Cropwell Bishop Creamery.

Stilton is thought to have first been developed in the villages of east Leicestershire and Rutland. It became famous early in the 18th century when Mrs Frances Pawlett, a dairywoman, entered into an arrangement with her brother-in-law Cooper Thornhill, who agreed to market her cheese. He was the owner of the Bell Inn at Stilton (now in Cambridgeshire). Cooper introduced the cheese to travellers staying at his busy inn. So the cheese has been named after the town in which it was sold and distributed, rather than the town where it was made. In fact, Stilton has never been made in Stilton.

Stilton Cheese Shutterstock/Jo Gough

Blue Stilton's distinctive blue veins are created by piercing the crust of the cheese with stainless steel needles, allowing air to come into the core. The manufacturing and ripening process takes approximately nine to twelve weeks. A 16-pound Stilton cheese takes 17 gallons of milk to produce. It must be of a cylindrical shape and form its own crust or coat. George Orwell defended English cooking and argued that Stilton was the best cheese of its type in the world.

Blewits

Blewits are wild mushrooms common throughout Nottinghamshire. They are very popular, particularly around autumn and during Goose Fair. They are also known as 'blue buttons', 'blue stalks', 'blue tails', 'bluewest' and 'blueys', due to the lilac-blue tinge they have when young. Although safe to eat, they should never be eaten raw as they can cause allergic reactions or indigestion. They have an intense, spicy flavour. One of the traditional local ways of cooking them is to stew them gently in milk and then thicken the liquid to make a sauce to serve them in, typically eaten with mashed tates. Foraging food was long considered a way to save money, and this was combined with buying economical cuts of meat – including offal, off-cuts and cheap parts of the animal. Traditional dishes using such ingredients include cow heel jelly, pigs' trotters, tripe, faggots and haslet. Faggots are traditionally made from pig's heart, liver and fatty belly meat or bacon minced together, with herbs and breadcrumbs added for flavouring. Locally, faggots are known as savoury ducks. Haslet is a type of meat loaf, cut into slices and eaten cold.

Work and Industry

Farming and agriculture have always been important in Nottinghamshire. In Norman times the county developed malting and wool industries. During the Industrial Revolution the county was important as it contained much-needed minerals such as coal and iron ore. The construction of canals and railways resulted in the improved movement of goods and exports, and the lace and cotton industries grew. In the 18th and 19th centuries deeper, mechanised collieries opened and mining became an important economic sector, although this declined after the 1984–85 miners' strike.

Following the invention of new frame machines, the county, in particular Nottingham, became synonymous with the lace industry. Factories such as Boots, Raleigh and John Player's were important employers in other industrial sectors.

Agriculture

The land of Nottinghamshire, with its river valley and

slopes, offered good soil to work. The earliest remaining evidence of farming in the region dates from Roman times. There is evidence showing that the Romans bridged the Trent and built villas with land for farming around Thurgarton, Southwell and Cromwell. Grain was grown for export, as well as beans, rye and oats for the farmers' own use and for feeding animals. Although cattle rearing was long developed before this time, shortly after the time of the Roman conquest cattle and sheep farming increased with the animals being used for meat, wool and milk. After this time, the Angles, Saxons and Danes worked their way from the east coast to the Trent Valley.

It is unknown whether the open-field system was brought over by these groups of peoples or whether it was already developing gradually during the period between the sixth and eleventh centuries. By the twelfth century most of Nottinghamshire's arable land was farmed on the open-field system. There is still one village in Nottinghamshire today that uses this method of farming and shows us how this worked throughout the county. This is Laxton. Here fields were divided into strips, and these strips were farmed in common among the landowners of the village. Laxton is unique because the open-field system is still alive and in daily use. Although Laxton is now recognised as an important heritage site, it is still home to working farmers, who rely on the land for their income. All the farmers in the village own land outside the open fields, but these open fields are not part of a museum or showcase; they are a living part of the agricultural landscape.

Such a traditional way of life has resulted in a distinct local vocabulary, from names for equipment and jobs such as bird tenting and brushing to distinctive ways of calling animals and animal calls. In Nottinghamshire, cows and bulls blooer and to call a sheep a farmer would say Come yowe! It would have to be cup cup for a horse, otch otch for chickens and cush cush for the cows. Chickens live in a fahl-ahse and sheep are gimmers.

Here a farm boy born in 1905 talks about the farmer he worked for:

He used to sit down for his breakfast about 9 o'clock and he always used to bring some wine with him and often it was elderberry wine, he used to leave me a drop in the bottle every day when he went back, he used to go then at dinnertime, he used to clear off and help to milk cus in those days they had to milk each individual cow, and then he used to send me into the fields turning hay and clover and all that for drying, cus you had to those days you know, go along turning it over, there were no machinery, they'd got a bit of machinery, horse machinery, like rakes and horse rakes and all such as that, and on these things what would turn it over you used to have to turn it over with a fork.

(Extract taken from A38 in Nottingham Local Studies Library, Oral History Collection)

Coal Mining

A Nottinghamshire miner born in 1911 explains:

I did nearly every job there while I was down the pit a bit at a time to get used to it, nearly every job. I even turned coal, datalling, helped to pack, that's datalling and knocked stuff down and put in to what you call a gob hole, like a bit of a road like a big ... well, you chucked all your rammel in there ... you see when you fetched the roof down to repack it, you kept out the road, well as you cleared it you couldn't put all that back, you chucked it down what you call 'gob holes' it's a road where they'd finished you see and you sort of helped pack it up with all this stuff.

(Extract taken from A15 in Nottingham Local Studies Library, Oral History Collection)

The East Midlands has a long history of mining activity, which can be dated back to the Romans, who mined lead in Derbyshire. Many mines in Nottinghamshire had the advantage of being close to the River Trent, which was the only navigable waterway in the county until canals were cut in the late 18th century. From about the middle of the 16th century the demand for coal rose rapidly, mainly because of scarcity of wood. This quickening of demand stimulated technological developments and the pits developed in a major way in the 19th and 20th centuries, with collieries increasing in size as deeper pits were sunk in more concealed coalfields rather than in the earlier exposed, shallower seams. From 1550 to 1950 the extent of coal extraction in the UK and those employed expanded at a colossal rate. In 1550 approximately 15,000 tons of coal were mined in the East Midlands. By 1950 this had expanded to 21,600,000 tons. The peak in output is thought to have been just before World War I. The increase of output from the collieries linked to the increase in workforce had huge effects on surrounding villages. Mining villages all around Nottinghamshire saw large population explosions and large population shifts as miners were frequently moved around the country.

The region led the way in innovations and technological advances in the coal industry, for example the use of railways to transport coal. To transport coal on a cost-effective basis the infrastructure needed to change dramatically. A traditional problem of East Midlands coalfields was that they could only supply local markets and could not compete with the sea-transported coal of the North-East. Canals could not cope, so trams and railways came into being to move coal from colliery to user. Canal, tramway and rail links helped the East Midlands supply further outlying areas such as London and many new settlements were developed to keep up with demand. Coal was the bedrock on which two of the largest and most profitable railway companies, the Midland Railway and the North Eastern Railways, built their business.

Headstock at Clipstone Colliery Shutterstock/daseaford

Also, as many of the larger collieries in the region were sunk in the late 20th century, many of the Nottinghamshire mines were leading coalfields in terms of technology. Thoresby was the earliest mine in the county to be completely powered by electricity, and it was the pioneering colliery in terms of mechanised production. Thoresby was also the first pit to turn over a million tons of coal per year. By the late 1980s it was producing over two million tons of coal. This also meant that many men from around the country moved to Nottinghamshire when other mines closed. A song in County Durham goes:

Leave your picks behind ye, ye'll no need them agen,
And off you go to Nottingham, join Robin's Merry Men.
Leave your cares behind ye, your future has been planned,
And off ye go tae Nottingham, tae Robin's promised land.

However, Thoresby is set to close in July 2015 and so the last remaining pit in Nottinghamshire – and the East Midlands for that matter – will disappear. With this, pit talk, the language needed dahn t'pit, is also in danger of disappearing and the mining meanings for words such as butty, bank, cage, cleat, firedamp, nuts, peas and togs are in danger of being lost for ever. Some mining terms are used more widely, and people in Nottinghamshire are often heard talking about snap time and what they are having for their snap.

Boots

We are not talking here about footwear – boot-making was the speciality of Leicester – this is about a chemists,

Boots UK, formerly known as Boots the Chemist, which was established in 1849 by JOHN BOOT, an agricultural worker. With the help of his family, he collected herbs in the fields around Nottingham in order to make herbal remedies. He opened a small herbalist store on Goose Gate in Nottingham in 1849, from which he prepared and sold herbal remedies. After his father's death in 1860, JESSE BOOT, aged 10, helped his mother to run the family's herbal medicine shop, which became Boot and Co. Ltd in 1883, then Boots Pure Drug Company Ltd in 1888.

The family wanted to bring affordable healthcare to the people and were becoming aware of other non-herbal remedies which were being produced. Most people struggled to be able to afford doctors' visits or medicines. By buying straight from the manufacturers, Jesse Boot was able to reduce the costs of medicines and prescriptions. He expanded the range of products he sold to include a variety of medicines and household necessities. He adopted a strategy of buying stock in bulk and selling his goods much cheaper than his competitors, advertising under the slogan 'Health for a Shilling'.

In 1884 Jesse transformed his business into a modern pharmacy and cut the price of prescriptions to half of what other people were charging. He opened branches in Lincoln and Sheffield – each one with a fully-trained pharmacist in store. It was the beginning of modern-day Boots. The wellbeing of employees was very important to Jesse. He provided welfare, education, sports and social facilities for the growing retail and manufacturing workforce. In 1895 he set up a laboratory and research centre to test products. During World War I Boots' growth accelerated. Until then, many pharmacy businesses had simply bought drugs like aspirin from Germany. With the outbreak of war that supply had suddenly dried up, and they were faced with finding other sources. Jesse set up a chemical department in 1915, staffed by scientists, specifically to create Boots' own products.

In 1920 Jesse Boot sold the company to the American United Drug Company. However, because of deteriorating economic circumstances in North America, Boots was sold back into British hands in 1933. The grandson of the founder, John Boot, who inherited the title Baron Trent from his father, headed the company. During the 1950s, Boots' scientists began developing an anti-inflammatory drug intended to have wide usage among the public. What they came up with – ibuprofen – certainly did the job. Ibuprofen was launched on to the market in 1969, with an over-the-counter version available from 1983.

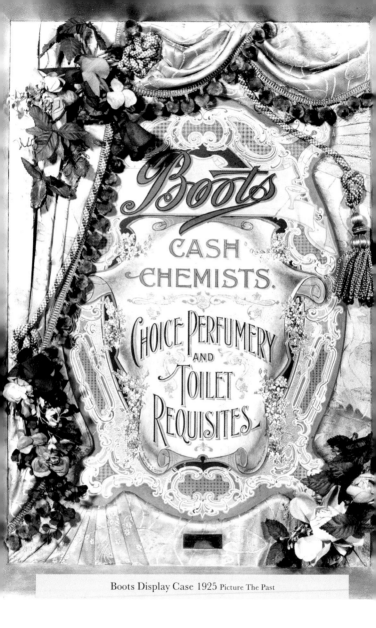

Boots Display Case 1925 Picture The Past

So, from that one store in Nottingham, the number of outlets increased to ten by 1890 and to an empire of over 550 shops by 1914. Today, Boots has 180 scientists working in laboratories in Nottingham. The company employs over 108,000 staff in more than 3,150 shops in over 20 countries worldwide. I think it is fair to say John and Jesse would be *reet chuffed!*

Lace
During the days of the British Empire Nottingham was the heart of the world's lace industry. The city is full of impressive examples of 19th-century industrial architecture, parts of which form part of a protected heritage area. Lace has been made by hand in England since the 16th century. Some of this was needle-made, but 'pillow' or 'bobbin' lace was more important and this was produced on a commercial basis in Nottinghamshire. Early lace net frames were operated by hand. The production unit was the home, often an upstairs room occupying the whole of the attic floor, or a workshop within the house. Usually the whole family was involved. The men worked the frame, while the women and children carried out other tasks, such as preparing thread or embroidering net.

Lace made by machine has been prominent among the industries of Nottingham since the 1760s. The earliest patent for making a lace fabric on a stocking frame was taken out by a stocking-maker called Butterworth, from near Mansfield. ROBERT FROST of Nottingham invented the first patterned lace machine. The invention of the knitting frame by WILLIAM LEE of Calverton in Nottinghamshire radically changed the process. It eventually gave the Lace Market in Nottingham its name. RICHARD ARKWRIGHT established a small cotton mill in Hockley in 1768. This led to the development of back-to-back housing accommodation for mill workers. JOHN HEATHCOAT, in 1808, was working in Nottingham while patenting the first machine capable of making lace that looked like hand-made pillow lace. His work was carried out in Nottingham and Loughborough and this machine was often referred to as 'Old Loughborough'. Lace made in this way was referred to as 'Nottingham Lace' to distinguish it from other, inferior, kinds of lace, but since this time any lace made by machine is called Nottingham Lace.

The lace industry was made up of different subgroups: the actual lace making itself, lace manufacturing (the finishing off process), lace dyeing and lace machine building. After the Nottingham city boundaries were extended in 1877 the lace industry could expand. At its peak in the early 1900s the sector employed more than 60,000 workers and thousands of machines.

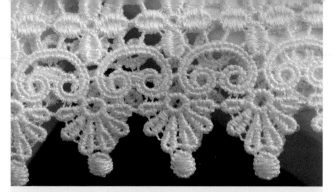

A fine example of the intricate work of Nottingham Lace
Norma Braber-McKinney

The area still called the Lace Market in Nottingham housed the lace manufacturers. Much of the other work took place in villages outside the town, such as Basford, Radford and Lenton. Very little of this industry remains, mainly some Victorian warehouses in the Lace Market. Many framework houses were also in Ruddington, where you can still find the Framework Knitters Museum.

Some workers were known as 'middle women', who would have groups of women working for them to deliver large bundles or work, and one woman explains how she got this post:

I'd just go to a firm and apply, say 'Are you needing a middle-woman'. I've got plenty of hands, they call them. They used to say how many hands have you got. That was a saying in the trade, used to say 'I've got 15 or 20 hands and can get your work through', and if they needed you, if there was a boom they'll need you, but that's how it'd happen.

(Extract taken from A85 in Nottingham Local Studies Library, Oral History Collection)

Sports and Recreation

As well as working hard, Nottinghamshire people have pastimes which they are famous for – the football and cricket teams are renowned, there are horse and dog racing grounds, you can find plenty of theatres and arenas, ice skating and ice hockey are popular, and plenty of water sports are based both on the River Trent and in the National Watersports Centre at Holme Pierrepont, which is the home of British canoeing. Aside from such sporting activities, there are numerous restaurants and pubs. Events include Goose Fair, which is a highly anticipated highlight. Many celebrities linked to Nottinghamshire have sporting associations. People like Brian Clough, Harold Larwood and Bill Voce will always be associated with Nottinghamshire – 'Cloughy' has a statue in Nottingham City Centre and the Larwood and Voce is a popular pub right next to Trent Bridge Cricket Club in West Bridgford.

There are also games which children liked to play, such as 'Rum-stick-a-bum', as explained by a man born in 1911:

> *Well, there'd be about eight on yer each side, one ud stand up agen the wall and all the others used to, same as a rugby scrum one ud get down and the next and the next till they was about half way across the road, and you had to, you'd all got to jump and they'd hode yer and if you touched the floor you was off, it was their turn*

and you got the best jumper to go fust to get right at the top as far as he could and then as you went they'd be just on the last man and then somebody get on top of him and on top of him and they'd give way then, then it'd start all ovver again, it was really good, it learnt you to jump you didn't arf used to fly through the air, leap frog an all, I could jump ote with leap frog, don't care how high the post. I even went ovver the top of a pillar box once, I only did it once!

(Extract taken from A15 in Nottingham Local Studies Library, Oral History Collection)

Football

Football is very important in Nottinghamshire, and Nottingham is the smallest city ever to boast a European Cup winning team. There are two football teams in Nottingham itself. Nottingham Forest Football Club, often referred to as Forest or The Reds, currently play in the Football League Championship. They have played at Sitti Grahnd (the City Ground) since 1898. The club was founded in 1865, were founder members of the Football Alliance in 1889, and joined the Football League in 1892. Nottingham Forest have worn red since the club's foundation. At the meeting in the Clinton Arms, which established Nottingham Forest as a football club, the committee passed a resolution that the team colours should be 'Garibaldi red'. This decision was made in honour of GIUSEPPE GARIBALDI, the Italian patriot who was the leader of the redshirts party. At this time, clubs identified themselves more by their headgear than their shirts and a dozen red caps with tassels were bought, making Forest the first club to 'officially' wear red, a colour that has since been adopted by a significant number of others. Forest is even the reason behind Arsenal's choice of red, having donated a full set of red kits following Arsenal's foundation in 1886.

Forest claimed their first major honour when they won the 1898 FA Cup, beating Derby County 3–1 at Crystal Palace. They won the cup again in 1959, beating Luton Town at Wembley. Their most successful period was under the management of BRIAN CLOUGH between 1975 and 1993, winning the League, back-to-back European Cups, four League Cups and two Full Members Cups. Nottingham Forest became one of the few teams – and the most recent one to date – to win the English First Division Championship a year after winning promotion from the English Second Division (1977–78 season). In July 2012, The Al-Hasawi family, from Kuwait, bought the club.

The Brian Clough sculpture on the junction of King Street
and Queen Street Norma Braber-McKinney

Notts County, just across the River Trent, are the closest professional football rivals geographically. However, Forest have remained at least one division higher than Notts since the 1994–95 season and Forest's fiercest rival is therefore Derby County, located 14 miles away. The two clubs contest the East Midlands derby, a fixture which has taken on even greater significance since the inception of the Brian Clough Trophy in 2007. Leicester City are another East Midlands rival due to the close proximity of the two cities. Sheffield United, based in South Yorkshire, is also too close for comfort – the rivalry has roots in the UK miners' strike of 1984–85, when the miners of South Yorkshire walked out on long strikes but the Notts Miners, who insisted on holding a ballot, continued to work.

Notts County Football Club, known as The Magpies because of their black and white striped shirts, was formed on 28 November 1862. They are the oldest football team in the world to currently play at a professional level. In 1888, Notts County, along with eleven other football clubs, became founding members of The Football League. They finished their first league season in 11th place, but just managed to avoid the wooden spoon, which went to Midlands rivals Stoke. However, Notts County did achieve their highest ever league finish of third in 1890–91, an achievement they repeated ten seasons later.

Between 1888–89 and 2013–14 Notts played a total of 4,756 Football League matches, which is more than any other English team. They currently play in League One of The Football League, the third tier in the English football league system. They kick off at Meddalain (Meadow Lane), just next to Sitti Grahnd and the Trent. The club has had several spells in the top division of English football, most recently in 1991–92, when County played in the old First Division.

These two teams aren't the only ones in the county, however, and Mansfield's Stags, Worksop Town's Tigers, Newark's Blues, Cranwell's Poachers, Newark and Radcliffe's Lions and Hucknall Colliery Welfare club have brought many people hours of joy and sadness over the years!

Cricket

Quintessentially English – and of worldwide fame of course – is cricket in Nottingham, and in particular Trent Bridge. It is home to Nottinghamshire County Cricket Club. Trent Bridge was first used as a cricket ground in the 1830s. The very first local cricket matches were held within the city walls, which meant that the cricketers could not charge admission as the ground was owned by the City Council. This changed when, in December 1837, the captain and self-appointed manager of the Nottinghamshire team,

WILLIAM CLARKE, married the landlady of the inn situated to the south of the bridge over the Trent, known as the Trent Bridge Inn. The following spring William laid a cricket ground in the meadow attached to the inn.

Trent Bridge Cricket Ground Shutterstock/mitzy

The first recorded cricket match there was held on an area of ground behind the Trent Bridge Inn in 1838, but Clarke found that there was not much interest in the sport at this time. However, over the years interest increased so much that in 1872 the county club were in a position to erect a much more elaborate pavilion on the opposite side of the ground from the inn. The successes continued, so much so that within ten years the new pavilion was found to be totally inadequate. The County Committee took the lease of a further two acres at the rear of the pavilion and in 1886 built the then largest pavilion in England. It hosted its first Test match in 1899, with England playing against Australia.

The ground used to be the shared home of Nottinghamshire County Cricket Club and Notts County Football Club, but as far back as 1910 the football and cricket seasons were considered to have become too overlapped, so the football club moved a couple of hundred yards away to Meadow Lane. Football was not the only other purpose of Trent Bridge. In the First World War the pavilion was used as a military hospital. During the Second World War, the Army occupied the pavilion, utilising it as the central mail sorting office – although matches were still played on the ground. The only bomb damage inflicted on Trent Bridge in the 1939–45 conflict was a direct hit on a single-storey building adjoining the indoor nets, used by the local Boys' Brigade. However, the ground is not reckoned to be one of

England's luckiest. Of the forty-eight Test matches played there, England have won only thirteen, losing fourteen and drawing twenty-one.

Goose Fair

Every year, during the first week of October, the Goose Fair returns to Nottingham. It is one of only two established fairs in the United Kingdom to carry the name. The other is the smaller Goose or 'Goosey' Fair in Tavistock, Devon. Its name is thought to derive from the thousands of geese that used to be brought from Lincolnshire to be sold. It was also long known for its cheese market. However, it is now famous for the more than 500 rides and games which take place. The fair dates back more than 700 years. Most historians think that it probably started just after 1284, when the Charter of KING EDWARD I referred to city fairs in Nottingham. The Goose Fair was cancelled due to the bubonic plague in 1646 and again during the two World Wars in the 20th century. Up until 1927 the Fair was held on Market Square, but because of the redevelopment of the square, it moved to Forest Recreation Ground where it has been held ever since.

Since the 1960s, Goosey, a six feet (two metres) tall fibreglass and timber goose, has come annually out of hibernation. This icon of the annual Goose Fair sits on the roundabout on Mansfield Road. With the geese and the cheese, food is an important element of Goose Fair. Another traditional feature is the mushy peas and mint sauce – forpni mix when served with chips, cobs with all sorts of fillings, tuffeys, tuffey apples, cocks on sticks and of course oakeys.

Although Goose Fair is undoubtedly the biggest and most famous fair in Nottinghamshire, there are plenty of other shows such as the agricultural Nottinghamshire County Show in Newark with livestock, food and farming machinery to entertain the whole family. One market worker explains the importance of the animal market at the Fair:

> *It was enormously popular at one time. Flakes, that is the wooden hurdles, were erected in roadways to provide extra pennage and great quantities of sheep, lambs, rams, were sold in the market on Goose Fair Day. I can remember we used to have to make special provision in the refreshment rooms, which were operated by the Department for some time. The refreshment room had to lay in fresh stocks of whisky and rum and so forth to cope with the great crowds which surged in on Goose Fair Day.*

(Extract taken from A74 in Nottingham Local Studies Library, Oral History Collection)

Famous Pubs

There are certainly too many famous pubs in the county to talk about here – you can find whole books written entirely about pub names in Nottinghamshire, so here is just a mention of some of the most well-known watering holes.

Ye Olde Trip Shutterstock/Guy Erwood

Several pubs in Nottingham claim to be 'England's Oldest Pub'. The Trip (Ye Olde Trip to Jerusalem) is partially built into the cave system below the Castle. It is said to have been established in 1189 and bears a sign stating that it is 'The Oldest Inn in England – 1189'. Legend has it that knights who answered the calls of Richard I to join the crusades stopped off here for a pint on their way to Jerusalem. It is even claimed that Richard himself frequented the pub, but this is probably merely legend, because the king spent little time in the country. The Salutation (Ye Olde Salutation Inn) on Maid Marian Way disputes the claim of age, as does The Bell Inn on the Old Market Square. So who is the oldest? It seems there is no straightforward answer. The Trip does have the oldest building, but it was for many years used as a brewery. The Salutation sits on the oldest recognised public house site, but it is a relatively new building. And The Bell Inn has the oldest public house building.

The Saracen's Head in Southwell is said to be the place where King Charles I spent his last night as a free man in May 1646. It is said that Oliver Cromwell later stayed in this same inn. Beeston is known for the variety of its traditional public houses. It has one of the highest concentrations of pubs-per-person in the United Kingdom. Many pubs in the region reflect the typical industry and pastimes of the people living here, with names such as The Test Match, The Magpies, The Sherwood and Little John Inn.

In order to keep all these pubs in ale (and not *mazzi-watter!*) Nottingham is home to its own brewery, Castle Rock Brewery. It was set up in 1977 and brews beers such as

Sheriff's Tipple. Many pubs in Nottingham still keep their beer in the cave cellars which Nottingham is famous for. There is also an annual beer festival called the Robin Hood Beer Festival which is always a sell-out.

The Trent

The watter of the Trent is everywhere in Nottinghamshire, from place names, pub names, company names, a University name and a cricket ground to local phrases. The name comes from the Celtic word for 'Trespasser' as it floods so often. It is one of the major rivers of England with its source in Staffordshire on the southern edge of Biddulph Moor just north of Stoke-on-Trent. It flows through the Midlands until it joins the River Ouse at Trent Falls to form the Humber Estuary, which empties into the North Sea between Hull and Immingham. The Trent is frequently considered an important divide between the North and the South of England, which is particularly interesting for Nottinghamshire, because the county lies on either side of this boundary. This sentiment was expressed in 1622 by MICHAEL DRAYTON in the poem Poly-Olbion:

> *And of the British floods, though but the third I be,*
> *Yet Thames and Severne both in this come short of me,*
> *For that I am the mere of England, that divides*
> *The north part from the south, on my so either sides,*

That reckoning how these tracts in compasse be extent,
Men bound them on the north, or on the south of Trent.

The Trent was crucial for the development of trade in the region, because it was the only navigable waterway in the county until the canals were built in the late 18th century. Prior to the mid-18th century there were few permanent crossings of the river, with only two bridges in the county: at Nottingham and Newark. There were, however, many ferries that operated along its course. These locations are indicated by the suffix 'ford' in place names such as Bridgford and Wilford.

An early view of Trent Bridge Picture the Past

The river is widely used for recreational activities, both on the water and along its riverbanks. You can follow many walking and cycle paths along the river, with plenty of refreshment stops on the way. Swimming in the river was popular in days gone by. In 1770 there were two bathing areas on opposite banks at Trent Bridge, which were improved in 1857 with changing sheds and an assistant. Similar facilities were present in 1870 on the water meadows at Burton-on-Trent, which also had its own swimming club. The river is used by all sorts of boats – from pleasure trips to canoes and motor boats. Many sights of Nottinghamshire can be viewed from the river. In fact, if you don't have a good time there, well, *Ah'll go to Trent!*

Children paddling in one of the pools alongside the river Trent
Picture the Past

Robin Hood

No book on Nottinghamshire would be complete without mentioning its most famous inhabitant. But who is Robin Hood? Is it a seven-foot (two metre) statue sculpted by JAMES WOODFORD out of bronze, weighing half a ton, which was presented to Princess Elizabeth and the Duke of Edinburgh in 1949? This sculpture is visited by many people during a visit to Nottingham, as it can now be found just outside the Castle, together with other statues of his outlaw comrades, also known as his *Merry Men* (LITTLE JOHN, FRIAR TUCK, WILL STUTELY, WILL SCARLET AND ALAN-A-DALE). But who is the real Robin Hood? We will probably never know for sure. He is variously said to have been a nobleman, a peasant or a fictional character. He has been referred to as ROBIN OF BARNSDALE, ROBIN OF LOXLEY and ROBIN OF SHERWOOD.

As long ago as the 15th century, Robin's story had made him infamous, as can be seen in this ballad of that time:

Lythe and listen Gentlemen
Who be of Free born blood
I will tell you of a bold yeoman
His name was Robin Hood.

It is thought that Robin Hood lived at the time of Richard

the Lionheart. And while the king was fighting in the crusades, his wicked brother Prince John wreaked havoc at home, taxing the people of England with help of men such as the Sheriff of Nottingham. Outlaws like Robin Hood helped the poor by punishing and stealing from the rich and giving it to the less well-off.

Since this time, books and films about the mysterious outlaw have fascinated young and old alike. Many actors have played Robin Hood, including ERROL FLYNN, SEAN CONNERY, KEVIN COSTNER and RUSSELL CROWE. Many locals have questioned the accuracy (or more pointedly the lack of correctness) of the Nottinghamshire dialect used by these actors, although it is important to bear in mind that the English spoken during this period would have been very different to the English we know today. In any case, there have also been numerous TV series, foreign films, spoofs and even a Disney film on our hero in which he is portrayed as a fox.

Many parts of Nottinghamshire are associated with Robin Hood, none more so than Sherwood Forest and the Major Oak, Robin Hood's Well, located near Newstead Abbey (within the boundaries of Sherwood Forest), and the Church of St Mary in the village of Edwinstowe. The Major Oak was said to have been a hiding place for Robin and his Merry Men, but recent dating of the tree shows that this cannot have been the case. There is a Robin Hood trail and associated activities and a Robin Hood tour through Nottingham. There are even roads such as Maid Marian Way that are associated with the legend in the city.

Regardless of the truth behind the Robin Hood story, such a folk hero continues to inspire people around the world. Many empathise with the sentiments surrounding his values. It seems apt to end with a line from the latest incarnation of Robin Hood, from RIDLEY SCOTT'S 2010 film starring RUSSELL CROWE, where he states:

There is no difference between a knight and any other man aside from what he wears.

A modern day Robin Hood in the streets of Nottingham
Norma Braber-McKinney

Select Bibliography

Books on Nottinghamshire dialect

BEETON, JOHN. *Nottingham As It Is Spoke, volumes 1–4*. Nottingham: JB Enterprises.

JAMES, JOY. 2008. *Yo'd mek a parson swear.* Nottingham: Mintas.

James, Joy. 2009. *Bog all to swear about!* Nottingham: Mintas.

SCOLLINS, RICHARD & JOHN TITFORD. 2000. *Ey up mi duck! Dialect of Derbyshire and the East Midlands.* Newbury: Countryside Books.

WRIGHT, PETER. 1979. *The Notts Natter. How it is spoke.* Keighley: Dalesman Books.

Internet resources on Nottinghamsire dialect

Our Nottinghamshire: A Community History Website. Dictionary: http://www.ournottinghamshire.org.uk/category_id__63.aspx

Information on BBC about Nottingham and Nottinghamese: http://www.bbc.co.uk/nottingham/content/articles/2005/01/04/features_about_nottinghamshire_nottinghamese_by_john_beeton_feature.shtml

Visit the British Library's 'Sound Archives' – each of their 'Accents and Dialects' Collections have annotated recordings from Nottinghamshire. The 'Survey of English Dialects' has recordings made between 1951 and 1974; the 'Millennium Memory Bank' has recordings from 1998 to

1999 and 'BBC Voices' has recordings made by local radio stations in 2005: http://sounds.bl.uk/Accents-and-dialects

It is also worth visiting the website 'Experience Nottinghamshire' which gives information about many facts of Nottinghamshire life and events: http://www.experiencenottinghamshire.com

Other publications of Nottinghamshire interest

ABRAHAMSON, MIKE. 2010. *Historic Britain: Nottinghamshire*. Stroud: The History Press.

BRIGGS-GOODE, AMANDA AND DEBORAH DEAN (EDS.). 2013. *Lace Here Now.* London: Black Dog Publishing. Harwood, Elain. 2008. Nottingham. London: Yale University Press.

HICKMAN, TREVOR. 1995. *The History of Stilton Cheese*. Stroud: Alan Sutton Publishing.

LYTH, PHILIP. 1989. *A History of Nottinghamshire Farming*. Newark: The Cromwell Press.

OLDFIELD, GEOFFREY. 1992. *Nottinghamshire Curiosities*. Dorset: The Dovecot Press.

OLDFIELD, GEOFFREY. 1998. *Nottinghamshire Inn Signs*. Nottingham: Technical Print Services.

POULTON-SMITH, ANTHONY. 2009. Nottinghamshire Place Names. Gloucestershire: The History Press.

SKINNER, JULIA. 2012. FLAVOURS OF NOTTINGHAMSHIRE. Recipes. Wiltshire: Frances Frith Collection.

Available now

Black Country Dialect

Bristol Dialect

Cockney Dialect

Cornish Dialect

Derbyshire Dialect

Devon Dialect

Essex Dialect

Glaswegian Dialect

Hampshire Dialect

Kentish Dialect

Lancashire Dialect

Liverpool Dialect

Manchester Dialect

Newcastle Dialect

Norfolk Dialect

Somerset Dialect

Suffolk Dialect

Sussex Dialect

Warwickshire Dialect

Yorkshire Dialect

Available in 2015

Evolving English WordBank

Lincolnshire Dialect

Dorset Dialect

Scottish Dialects

The Cotswolds Dialect

The Lake District Dialect

Wiltshire Dialect

Leicestershire Dialect

See website for more details: bradwellbooks.com